NEW ZEALAND

TIGER BOOKS INTERNATIONAL

Text
Colin Monteath

Graphic Design
Anna Galliani

Map
Arabella Lazzarin

Contents

1 *Rotorua in central North Island is one of the focal points for Maori culture in New Zealand. Carved doorways, weapons and waka canoes are a vital part of Maori tradition.*

2-3 *The Wanganui river is the longest continuously navigable river in New Zealand. With its headwaters on the central volcanic plateau of the North Island the Wanganui flows some 125 miles to the Tasman Sea. Once an important river for the Maoris commuting by canoe, it is now popular with recreationists keen on rafting, jet boating and canoeing. Some lovely peaceful campsites can be found in the heart of rich farmland bordering the river.*

4-5 *The Skyline Gondola whisks Queenstown visitors several hundred feet above the city to a restaurant and observation platform with a stunning panorama over Lake Wakatipu and the Remarkable Mountains. Queenstown is recognised as the fun capital of the South Island's "Southern Lakes" district with superb trekking and boating in summer and skiing for all levels of ability in winter. This view of Queenstown is taken in early autumn with the trees just starting to change colour and the first snowfall on the Remarkables.*

6-7 *New Zealand is known as the "Shaky Isles" and nowhere is the volcanic activity more spectacular or violent than on White Island , a small island some 30 miles north of the township of Whakatane in the Bay of Plenty. While the volcano is clearly visible from Whakatane, visitors can get a better feel for active vulcanism by taking a scenic flight in a small aircraft directly over the craters.*

8 *This aerial view of part of Northland's coastline, jutting into the Pacific Ocean gives a good impression of the remote and pristine beaches of clean white sand for which New Zealand has rightly become famous. Rugged headlands of dense bush come right down to the sea adding to the feel of isolation. Northland is easily accessible from the city of Auckland.*

9 *As the sun sinks into the Tasman Sea at the end of the day the western aspects of Mount Cook are transformed into a kaleidoscope of pinks and mauves. At 12,350 feet Mount Cook is New Zealand's highest peak. Although not high by world standards, its glaciated flanks descend into deep shadowy valleys not far above sea level. The Southern Alps stretch the length of South Island providing a mecca for mountaineers, skiers and trekkers.*

This edition published in 1995 by TIGER BOOKS INTERNATIONAL PLC , 26a York Street Twickenham TW1 3LJ, England.

First published by Edizioni White Star. Title of the original edition: Nuova Zelanda, il Paese dei grandi venti. © World copyright 1995 by Edizioni White Star, Via Candido Sassone 22/24, 13100 Vercelli, Italy.

ISBN 1-85501-669-9

Printed in Singapore by Tien Wah Press. Colour separations by La Cromografica, Ghemme (Novara) Italy.

11 *Aoraki (Mount Cook), right, and Mount Tasman, New Zealand's second highest summit, are perfectly reflected in a West Coast lake. The backbone of the Southern Alps is only about 12.5 miles from the Tasman Sea so steep glaciers such as the Fox and Franz Josef flow down through heavily vegetated gorges to the narrow coastal plain.*

12-13 *The tiny township of Lake Tekapo sits at the crossroads of the Mackenzie Country and the Southern Alps. Lake Tekapo is a popular recreation spot in both summer and winter. Its glacial fed waters feed the Benmore-Waitaki hydro-electric scheme providing electricity to much of the South Island. Lake Tekapo can be quite eye-catching as the sun reflects across water impregnated with fine glacial sediment thereby creating a vivid turquoise landscape.*

14-15 *A fleet of small ferries transport passengers and vehicles between the North and South Islands from Wellington to Picton across Cook Strait. It is a three-hour voyage at present although faster, more modern vessels will be in operation shortly. The Cook Strait has a wicked reputation for stormy weather although by the time vessels get close to Picton they are generally sheltered in the peaceful waters of Marlborough Sounds.*

16-17 *Lovely historic homes set in parklike gardens are a feature of New Zealand. Mansion House on Northland's Kawau Island was built by Governor Sir George Grey in 1862. Kawau Island is also the refuge for the tiny Parma wallaby thought to be close to extinction in its Australian homeland.*

18-19 *Lake Mangamahoe with its foreshores draped with tree ferns lies at the foot of the dormant volcano Taranaki (Mount Egmont). The Taranaki district with its fertile volcanic soil is famous for highly productive dairy farms. Taranaki is only a few miles from the Tasman Sea so often catches violent weather.*

Introduction

In 1884, the European Andreas Reischek, wrote of New Zealand "...and like a carpet at your feet, in endless gradations of light and shade, the New Zealand bush spreads out in green waves downwards to the edge of the ocean."

Even today, despite much of the country being heavily modified by agriculture and the vigorous growth of modern sprawling cities, New Zealand is blessed with vast areas of wild bushland, a rugged backbone of alpine peaks, volcanoes, hot springs, clean water and remote unfrequented beaches. New Zealand is home to a relic of the reptile world, the Tuatara, and strange flightless birds, notably the Kiwi and the nocturnal Kakapo, the largest parrot in the world. Seen by many as a haven of peace, New Zealand continues to thrive in a world racked by tension and overcrowding. While some merely focus attention on New Zealand's achievements in various international sporting fields, the tiny country has rocketed into prominence in the 1980s as a result of its nuclear-free policy. In general, New Zealanders care for their environment and take great pride in the maintenance of an extensive national park system. The World Heritage designation of South Westland is seen as a major wilderness of international significance. New Zealand's environmental management skills have become a highly sought-after commodity especially throughout South-East Asia.

As a tourist destination New Zealand is firmly on the map as a place for a quiet relaxing holiday at a coastal village or perhaps for a "farm-stay" experience on a high country sheep station. For the more adventurous who relish clean air and outdoor activities, New Zealand is a paradise for skiing, yachting, mountaineering, scuba-diving, kayaking and fishing. Many consider New Zealand as "the walking capital of the world" - a place to leave the automobile behind.

Separated from the ancient supercontinent Gondwanaland for the last 100 million years, New Zealand lies in isolation on the southern rim of the Pacific Ocean - a glittering necklace of verdant, tranquil islands inhabited by people of Maori,

Polynesian and European extraction.

New Zealand's nearest neighbour, Australia, lies to the west some 1,250 miles away across the storm-tossed Tasman Sea. New Zealand was originally connected to the eastern edge of the Australian mainland, Tasmania and Antarctica. With the gradual breaking up of Gondwanaland's land-links, New Zealand missed out on the introduction of the early marsupial mammals (Kangaroos, Koalas etc) which arrived in Australia via South America and on snakes which wriggled into Australia from New Guinea-Indonesia connections. Highly-specialised birds and unique plants are among New Zealand's most attractive legacy on land. Coastal waters abound in penguins, seals, whales and dolphins including the smallest dolphin in the world, the Hector's.

The Maoris have been called "Vikings of the Sunrise". These early Polynesian seafarers were skilful Pacific navigators who landed on the northern shores of New Zealand in ocean-going *wakas* (canoes) some 800 years before the arrival of the first European voyagers. Apart from Antarctica, New Zealand was the last major land mass to be reached and inhabited by man.

The Maori people gradually colonised the semi-tropical regions of the North Island, eking out an existence from hunting, fishing and harvesting the *kumara* (sweet potato). Tribal warfare and cannibalism were common. Weaker tribes were pushed southward to inhabit the much colder South Island. Many hunted the now-extinct Moa, a flightless ostrich-like creature, perhaps the tallest bird ever to have lived. While the precipitous Southern Alps proved a formidable barrier for the Maori, crossing routes were established to the rugged rainforest regions of the West Coast in search of *Pounamu*, the "stone of the gods" - a highly-prized nephritic jade.

Centred in Batavia (now Jakarta) in the 17th Century, the Dutch East India Company dominated the trading routes around the East Indies for 200 years. Voyages purely for exploration were rare. In 1642 Abel Tasman, in his wooden vessels *Zeehaen* and *Heemskerk*, sailed eastward at 55 S underneath mainland Australia searching for *Terra Australis Incognita* - the great south land - and a faster way to the lucrative trading markets in South America, then dominated by the Spanish.

Tasman discovered Van Dieman's Land (Tasmania) before crossing what is now known as

the Tasman Sea to reach the west coast of the South Island of New Zealand. On December 13th 1642 he recorded "a Land Uplifted High" in his log as he caught sight of the snowy summits of the Southern Alps which rise to 12,000 feet within about 15 miles of the bush-lined beaches. Thinking he had reached South America, Tasman named his landfall *Staten Landt* (the Dutch name for South America). Later, the name changed to *Niew Zeeland* after Tasman's native province.

Englishman James Cook opened up the Pacific to the European world with three remarkable voyages of scientific discovery in the 1700s. Captain Cook circumnavigated New Zealand in 1769 and formally took possession of the land for the British crown. Cook's excellent charts of the coastline were relied upon for the next 150 years despite his error of thinking Stewart Island was part of the South Island. Cook visited New Zealand twice more during the 1770s so he could resupply his ships after long arduous voyages to the edge of both polar regions. Although Tasman and Cook's first encounters with the Maoris were violent, Cook grew to respect Maori culture, making many friends during his ten year-association with the country.

Almost inevitably, Cook's journals sparked off the sealing and whaling industry in New Zealand waters. With Europe engulfed in the Napoleonic wars, demand for various byproducts of seals and whales grew steadily. Based out of eastern Australia, the renegade sealers used New Zealand harbours as a source of fresh water and timber to repair their ships. Initially seals were plentiful; however it wasn't long before numbers were sufficiently depleted to force the hunters further south to New Zealand's sub-antarctic islands.

Following the opening up of eastern Australia and Tasmania as penal colonies in the late 1700s large scale immigration to New Zealand from Britain got underway in 1842; formal annexation by Britain occurred in 1840 after the signing of the Treaty of Waitangi. The introduction of firearms, alcohol, prostitution and diseases by the new colonists had a profound effect on the Maori population, decimating their numbers. Despite some violent skirmishes (Maori Land Wars 1860-81) Maori and *Pakeha* (European) gradually learned to live peaceably enough together. The Maori had no concept of owning or selling their land and as a result many of the so-called

land deals are still being vigorously contested today by a well-educated and articulate Maori population. Maori today make up about ten per cent of New Zealand's population of 3.5 million and are flourishing in a proud revival of Maori tradition - *Maoritanga*.

Although considered a "young" country, 150 years of European settlement combined with a rich tapestry of Maori/Polynesian influence has created a multiracial New Zealand - a nation of pivotal importance in the Pacific basin.
Once solely dependent on its exports of wool, meat and dairy products to the British market, New Zealand has evolved as a modern exporting nation of primary produce on the world stage. Horticultural produce, notably the "Kiwi fruit", and an emerging wine industry have now established themselves as important revenue earners. New Zealand's climate can be considered "ideal" - ranging from semi-tropical in the far north to cool temperate in the south. Summers are never blisteringly hot and winters are relatively short and mild.

New Zealand is roughly the size of the United Kingdom; its three main islands (North, South and Stewart) result in a coastline which is over 6,200 miles long.
New Zealanders, although largely urbanites, are never far from the sea which provides a basis for both industry and recreation. Easy access to bush and mountain country for various forms of recreation is crucial to the well-being of all New Zealanders. From richly-grassed farmlands in the north to high country sheep stations in the south, farming traditions are deeply engrained in the "Kiwi" ethos. New Zealand is a compact land of tall Kauri forest, bubbling mud pools, mysterious forest-clad fiords and slender icy peaks - a special place that is a vital crossroads on the doorstep of both the Pacific and Antarctica.

With a centerpiece of the snow-capped active volcanoes, Ngauruhoe and Ruapehu, the North Island is a buckled landscape of fertile soils and bright green grasslands. The thermal region of the central volcanic plateau around Rotorua and Taupo is a focal point of Maori culture.
Two thirds of New Zealand's population, including over 90% of the Maoris, live in the North Island. New Zealand's biggest cities are in the north with Auckland (over 1 million inhabitants) sandwiched between Manukau and Waitemata harbours in Northland while the capital, Wellington, is

situated on the blustery southern tip of the island.

Auckland - the "City of Sails"- has every shape and size of craft taking to the water on weekends to enjoy cruising the network of waterways. Aucklanders relish the carnival atmosphere which exists when they play host to the crews of round-the world Whitbread yachts. Auckland has developed into an important centre for yacht design and boat-building. The city has a prosperous fast-growing feel to it and is recognised as the commercial capital of the country. Auckland was the official capital until 1865 when it was transferred to the more central Wellington. Sprawling suburbs mushroom across rolling hills from the city centre with neat rows of single-storey wood or brick houses criss-crossing the landscape. Most New Zealanders are lucky enough to own their own home and many take great pride in tending a colourful mosaic of flowers, shrubs and vegetables. For a city Auckland also has the largest concentration of Polynesians in the Pacific. As such the city provides a variety of important support systems for the many smaller island nations to the north.

Northland's Bay of Islands, Coromandel Peninsula and the Bay of Plenty are a big draw for both Aucklander and tourist alike. Clean beaches prove a popular attraction during the December-March summer months. Year-round however, sailing, scuba-diving and big game fishing entice enthusiasts to explore favourite haunts around the myriad of islands and channels. While Auckland can appear as busy as any big city, a relaxed outdoor life-style is still possible in the "winterless north".

The Waikato region of the central North Island with its principal city of Hamilton is the hub of New Zealand's dairy, sheep, horse and beef cattle-breeding industries. Many visitors marvel at the greenness of the grass. Despite the continuing importance of such traditional farming, vineyards and Kiwifruit orchards have significantly changed the appearance and economy of the rural scene in recent years.

The sacred peaks of Ngauruhoe, Tongariro and Ruapehu were gifted to the New Zealand people by a Maori chief in 1887 forming Tongariro National Park only 15 years after Yellowstone in USA, the first national park in the world. Every weekend from June to November winter sports fans flock from the major centres to the skifields clinging to the volcanic slopes of

Mount Ruapehu (about 9170 feet) with its simmering volcanic lake. Nearby, Lake Taupo, New Zealand's largest lake, was formed 1800 years ago by one of the biggest volcanic blasts in history. Ngauruhoe has violently erupted several times in recent decades, yet on the west coast, within sight of the Tongariro peaks, lies the slumbering ice-capped cone of Taranaki (Mount Egmont) a beautiful symmetrical volcano.

On the northern flank of Cook Strait, within sight of the South Island, Wellington sits nervously astride a major fault line which dissects the entire North Island. While New Zealand engineers have been highly innovative in strengthening buildings against earthquake damage it is the "Windy Wellington" reputation which seems to be of more pressing concern to inhabitants on a daily basis. Stacked like toy blocks among thick clusters of native bush, Wellington's brightly painted wooden houses cling to the steep hillsides overlooking a fine harbour. Wellingtonians take a ringside seat to observe and debate the finer points of the government's stewardship of the nation.

The North Island is a dynamic landscape in the throes of constant change - the driving hub of New Zealand's social and economic evolution. For an entirely different pace of life, with smaller cosier cities, more varied and extreme forms of recreation in a wilder untamed landscape, it is necessary to take the three-hour ferry trip from Wellington and start a journey into the South Island.

The South Island is unlike its northern neighbour in almost every way. With a backbone of alpine peaks as glaciated and rugged as any on Earth, the Southern Alps influence most aspects of life in the south. Fast-flowing rivers gouge out the hillsides creating vast outwash plains of shingle. Fertile soils in the east enable grain crops to grow well while in the west luxuriant rainforest is a national treasure, connecting the mountains to the Tasman Sea only 12 miles away.

Christchurch (300,000 people) and Dunedin (200,000) on the east coast are the principal South Island cities and while there has been a definite "drift to the north" in recent years, with people looking for work, both cities are now thriving business and cultural centres with inspiring communal spirit.

Large sheep stations, with their wide-verandahed homesteads located at the head of beautiful river valleys, have been the main-stay of

South Island farming for generations. The high country autumn muster is an essential yet colourful event in the farming calendar. The shepherds on horseback (perhaps assisted by helicopters) drive the sheep down from the alpine tussock country to lower pastures before the onset of winter snowstorms.

The South Island has become well known as a fine producer of both apples and pears with prosperous orchards centred in the Nelson and Otago districts. Introduced deer bred quickly to become a pest throughout South Island forests, however, these days commercial deer farming for meat, hide, velvet and breeding stock is a major export earner.

Tourism is now the principal industry in the south with picturesque spots such as Queenstown attracting foreigners to the skifields above the town. The Southern Lakes of Wanaka, Wakatipu and Manapouri create endless opportunities for the boating enthusiast. The lakes also provide access to spectacular walking routes such as the Milford Track. Other tracks like the Routeburn, Keplar, Heaphy, Rees-Dart and Abel Tasman have now become as popular as the Milford for those wishing to sample the varied environments of the south. Excellent walking tracks are also a feature of Stewart Island which boasts the most likely chance of a visitor observing a Kiwi in the wild. Stewart Island is only a short ferry trip from Invercargill/Bluff at the southern tip of the South Island. With only 12 miles of roads, Stewart Island is an ideal spot to unwind for those stressed by the age of automobiles.

Fiordland National Park with famous landmarks Milford Sound and Mitre Peak is a truly remarkable wilderness of global importance. Whether viewed from the air or from a walking track, the deep sombre fiords with their outlets to the Tasman Sea have a majesty and serenity all of their own especially when blanketed by snow. The rain is measured in metres in Fiordland and while this can be a deterrent for some, storms are a time when the cliffs come alive with waterfalls, creating the most spectacular visual shows of light and water - nature at its best.

It knows how to rain on the West Coast as well, however: on a still peaceful morning in Fox Glacier, Westland has an intimacy and beauty that is unique. At the end of the day as the sun settles into the Tasman Sea, Mounts Cook and Tasman, New Zealand's highest summits, take on a deep

20-21 Evening light across Westhaven marina provides a peaceful foreground for Auckland's skyline of modern buildings. Auckland is often called "the yachting capital of the world" for its famous harbour enables sailors of all abilities to recreate or race to their hearts content. Auckland is the principal base for yachts preparing for long voyages into the Pacific.

22-23 Skiing on the big open glacial neves of the Southern Alps creates an amazing feeling of freedom. This skier is swooping across a crevasse bridge high on the Franz Josef Glacier of Westland National Park. The Tasman Sea is only a few miles away so it is very special to be in an alpine world yet look down vegetated gorges to surf crashing on a West Coast beach.

24-25 Lake Benmore in the centre of the South Island and the Waitaki river system's hydro-electric scheme provides an important source of electric power for much of New Zealand. Melt from the snow-covered foothills of the Southern Alps in the background keeps this beautiful lake topped up with water for much of the year.

26-27 Christchurch at dusk takes on a peaceful relaxed air. With 300,000 people, Christchurch is the largest city in the South Island and is an important focal point for the surrounding rural community on the Canterbury Plains. Spring in Christchurch is a special time. The city is filled with blossoms in the many tree-lined streets or carefully manicured private gardens, yet the nearby foothills of the Southern Alps are still draped with snow.

burgundy glow. Inexorably, the Fox and Franz Josef Glaciers grind their way down from the neves of the Main Divide. Their moraine-covered snouts crunch and shove a wall of ice to the verge of the rainforest - an ice-forest interface in a constant state of turmoil only a few miles from the beach.

On the drier eastern slopes of the loftiest peaks lies the famous Hermitage hotel and Mount Cook village - the principal mecca for mountaineers keen to test their ice skills. New Zealand's peaks are not high by world standards (Mount Cook is 12,350 feet); however when their heavily glaciated faces and ridges are pounded by bad weather coming in from the Tasman Sea they take on a fierceness which needs to be treated with respect and judgement. Visitors to the Hermitage are often privileged to witness spectacular mountain vistas as well as a never-ending kaleidoscope of curved wind clouds.

Only two hours north of Christchurch lies the tiny fishing village of Kaikoura which has now developed as the whale and dolphin watching centre of New Zealand. Sperm whales routinely come to feed on squid which thrive on the rich upwelling of nutrients off the edge of the Continental Shelf. Some visitors spend hours with the whales, bobbing around with a guide in an inflatable boat while others prefer to swim with the dolphins closer to the beach. Fur seals huff and snort on the rocky platform nearby.

New Zealand has changed much in the past 20 years and is now an active player on the world stage, voicing an opinion or taking action on matters of global politics, conflict and matters of international trade. At home New Zealanders enjoy an easy relaxed intimacy with their environment. They can also take the time to offer hospitality to a foreign guest or perhaps go out of their way to put the visitor on the right road. Both attributes are worth a good deal.

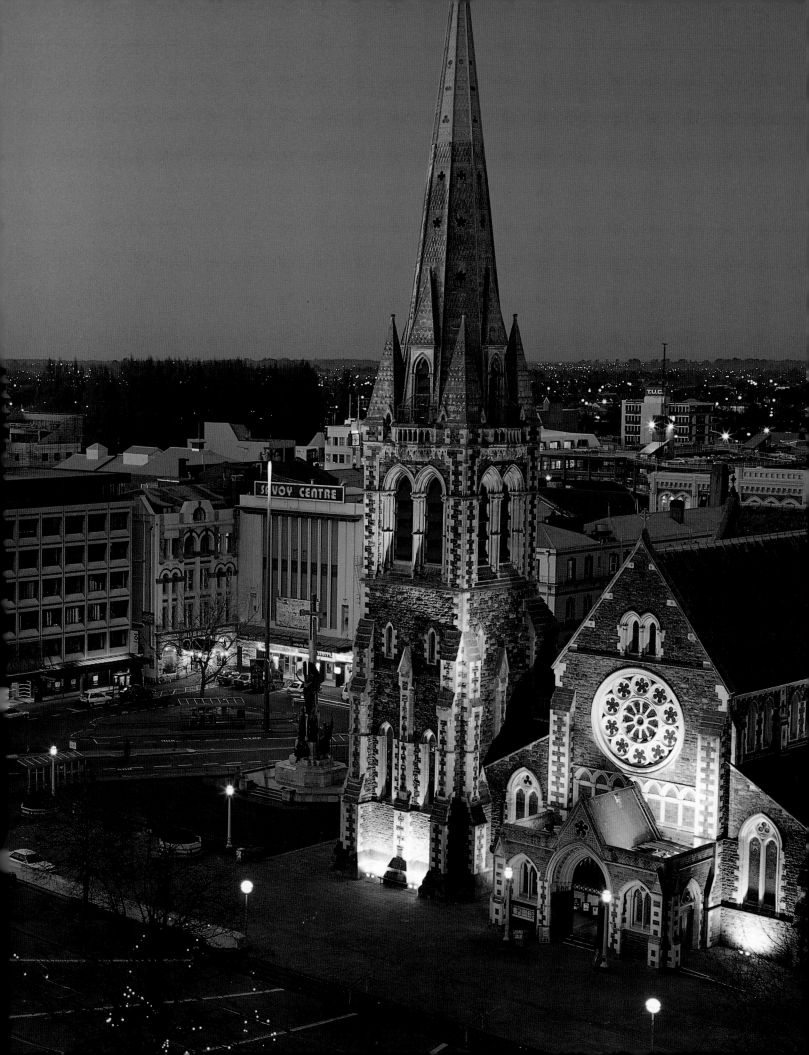

On the Southern Rim of the Pacific

28 top *Kaikoura harbour is the home port for many local fishing vessels which catch both fin fish and lobsters in the rich coastal waters of the Pacific. With a strong up-welling of nutrients where the continental shelf comes close to the township of Kaikoura many sperm whales come to feed. Whale watching and swimming with Hector's dolphins have put Kaikoura on the international map for all nature lovers.*

28 bottom *Heavy rain clouds drift down the Rees and Dart Valleys to blanket sheep paddocks on the fertile river flats at the head of Lake Wakatipu near the township of Glenorchy. With over 80 million sheep in New Zealand fine grades of wool for clothing and carpets as well as meat products have been the mainstay of the country for most of this century.*

29 *Sunset on Mount Tasman (foreground) and Aoraki (Mount Cook) lights up the summit icecaps of the two highest peaks in the Southern Alps. Mountaineers come from all over the world to test their skills on the steep ridges and faces of these peaks. Mount Cook and Westland National Parks lie on each side of these mountains and with easy road access and fine hotels everyone can enjoy the best of New Zealand's unique alpine scenery.*

Blessed with bushland
and alpine peaks

30 *Autumn colours light up the poplar trees on the shore of Lake Wanaka in the Southern Lakes district of the South Island. Wanaka is an important centre for outdoor recreation with good access to walking tracks, mountaineering, fishing, skiing and boating. Wanaka township is on the edge of Mount Aspiring National Park with its famous Routeburn Track.*

31 *North Canterbury's Waiau valley just north of Christchurch is a relaxing spot for a picnic or a walk in the surrounding forests to enjoy the autumn colours. Waiau's rolling hill country is ideal sheep and cattle country.*

32-33 *The simple stone Church of the Good Shepherd is in harmony with its alpine surroundings, the Two Thumb Range. Perched on the shores of the turquoise Lake Tekapo, the church's stained-glass window affords a stunning view of the Southern Alps.*

34-35 *This aerial view of a Kiwi fruit orchard in Takaka's Golden Bay region in the provence of Nelson illustrates the intensive nature of modern agriculture in New Zealand. Kiwi fruit has become an internationally important crop in the* last decade with many farmers in the north of the South Island and throughout the North Island planting orchards. The Golden Bay region is also a popular holiday spot and retreat for many skilled craft workers, notably potters.*

36-37 *An aerial view of the Canterbury Plains provides a graphic idea of the nature of the agriculture between the cities of Christchurch and Ashburton. Crops such as wheat, mustard, oats and barley thrive on the outwash plains fed by melt water from the Southern Alps.*

40-41 *The lush vegetation of Urewera National Park, on the North Island, offers an ideal habitat for cuckoos, tui kakas, and pigeons. The expanse of lakes and woodlands extends over a territory of fifty thousand acres, to the northeast of Hawke Bay and to the west of Poverty Bay.*

42-43 *Glenorchy township, tucked away at the head of Lake Wakatipu and only an hour's drive from Queenstown, is one of the most perfect weekend retreats in the South Island. It is the base for walking tracks into the Mount Aspiring National Park such as the Rees-Dart and Routeburn. Fishing, boating and horseriding are also popular with visitors to local hotels on the lake foreshore. Autumn is definitely one of the best times to visit with crisp mornings, warm windless days and lovely colours in the trees.*

38 *The meandering Waimakariri River flows out of Canterbury's Torlesse Range just north of Christchurch. Canterbury rivers are popular trout fishing spots. The braided channels are also a mecca for jet-boating enthusiasts who race their craft over the shallow though fast-flowing water at high speed. New Zealand engineers invented the jet boat, a craft which has now been exported all over the world.*

39 *Banks Peninsula is Christchurch's best-kept secret. Ancient volcanic rims and sunken calderas provide both rugged hilltops and safe secluded harbours. The tranquillity of Bank's Peninsula enchants all who visit. Sleepy little towns such as Akaroa with its early French influence make the peninsula a popular weekend retreat for Christchurch city dwellers.*

44 Manuska *is a small sailing craft which can be chartered from the township of Te Anau to visit many of the remote trekking and fishing havens on Lake Manapouri in Fiordland National Park. Te Anau is the base for trekkers commencing the famous Milford Track which connects Lake Manapouri with Milford Sound through some of the most spectacular alpine and forest scenery anywhere.*

45 *Tucked high among the peaks of rugged Fiordland National Park, Lake Quill overhangs densely vegetated valleys of the Milford Track. Sutherland Falls drop 1870 feet into Staircase Creek. Carved by ancient glaciers the U-shaped valley walls of Fiordland are quite remarkable. Sudden torrential rainfall is a feature of Fiordland which creates hundreds of spectacular waterfalls on the steep vegetated granite walls. Fiordland National Park is an important cornerstone of the South Westland World Heritage region.*

Forests, fronds and falls

46-47 *Purakanui Falls is one of many lovely waterfalls in the Catlins district of southern Otago. The Catlins not only provide really delightful forest walks but allow visitors to experience remote beaches on the South Island's south-east coast, the home of fur seals and yellow-eyed penguins.*

47 *The rain forest of Waipoua extends over an area of six thousand acres, and is one of the largest* kauri *pine forests in all of New Zealand.*

48-49 *South Westland's unique "World Heritage" region runs down most of the western side of the South Island. Pristine rainforest with tall tree ferns and tangled undergrowth is sandwiched between wild beaches and alpine peaks.*

Lakes, fiords and bush-clad coasts

50 *Window Rock at Rawhiti Point is typical of the rugged coastline around parts of the North Island's Bay of Islands. The 500-mile bush-clad coastline embraces 150 islands which impressed Captain Cook when he first sailed into the sheltered waters in 1769.*

51 *This aerial view of Russell in the Bay of Islands is typical of the small townships in Northland which attract many visitors keen on boating and water sports in the summer months from December to March.*

52-53 *The port of Picton on the northern tip of the South Island is the hub for rail and road transport meeting the ferries bound for Wellington, three hours away across Cook Strait.*
This aerial view gives a good impression of Picton's location on the edge of Queen Charlotte Sound. The Marlborough Sounds is a boating and fishing paradise for the many New Zealanders who have private holiday cottages or "batches" tucked away in the forest. Water taxis and float planes take visitors to the many beautiful lodges now developed in the region. The Queen Charlotte Walkway is becoming more popular with trekkers keen on an easy trail through tree fern forests with view down to beautiful waterways.

54 *The old steamboat* Earnslaw *with its polished brass and nuggety wooden fittings has been used on Lake Wakatipu since the 1920s. Initially used to service remote sheep stations further up the lake from Queenstown the* Earnslaw *is now used for tourist cruises on the lake. Passengers can get off at sheep stations to enjoy a cup of tea and scones with fresh cream and jam as well as to watch sheep being hand shorn.*

55 *Milford Sound is rightly famous all over the world for its superb boating excursions out past Mitre Peak and down heavily vegetated fiords to the edge of the Tasman Sea. Dolphins often frolic in the bow wave of the launches. The vessels thrill passengers by going underneath some of the many spectacular waterfalls which cascade down the granite rock faces.*

56 left *Cape Kidnapper's in Hawke Bay, near the North Island cities of Hastings and Napier, is a popular spot for those who wish to observe a gannet colony at close quarters.*

56 right *This aerial view of the Kaikoura Peninsula illustrates that even on the east coast of the South Island the mountains come down almost into the sea. Kaikoura is a small fishing port but is a focal point for breeding seals, sperm whales and dolphins.*

57 *Stewart Island is the third major island of New Zealand and it lies only a few miles south of the South Island across Foveaux Strait. With only a dozen miles of road on the whole island visitors explore the forests and bays on foot or by launch. Stewart Island forests are one of the best places to see the unique Kiwi, New Zealand's famous flightless bird. In many places the bush comes right down among the boulders on the beach allowing the visitor the experience the feeling of exploring while fossicking along the coast. Fishing, lobster, mussel and and salmon farming are the main industries on Stewart Island.*

58-59 *The moon-shaped Moeraki boulders emerge each day as the tide recedes on the south-east coast near Dunedin. Formed 60 million years ago the spherical boulders are formed by lime salts gradually solidifying around a small centre. Maori legend prefers to consider them the food baskets from a ship-wrecked canoe.*

59 *The layer-cake limestone rocks at Punakaiki on the West Coast north of Greymouth have been eroded in such a way that spectacular blowholes send incoming waves high into the air. It is really exciting to visit these "pancake" rocks when there is a storm out in the Tasman Sea.*

60-61 *Mitre Peak is perhaps the most famous mountain in Fiordland National Park. Its shape, together with the mirror-calm waters of Milford Sound, has become as well-known a symbol of*

New Zealand as the Kiwi. This view is taken from the lawn in front of the Milford Hotel, the base for all launch trips and scenic flights in the region.

62-63 *Nugget Point lighthouse on the Catlin's Coast south of Dunedin is one of the first places in New Zealand to witness the sunrise over the Pacific Ocean. Fur seals and yellow-eyed penguins inhabit the rocky beaches around the lighthouse.*

The icy heart of the South Island

64 *Sunset from the summit of Magellan Peak in Westland National Park lights up the short steep glaciers which curl down into the West Coast forested valleys. The Southern Alps run the complete length of the South Island and in places are no more than 12.5 miles from the beaches on the fringe of the Tasman Sea. A massive alpine fault runs through the alps with associated hot springs providing a welcome bath for weary climbers and trekkers.*

65 *Evening light illuminates the western side of Aoraki (Mount Cook) and some of the lower peaks of the Balfour and La Perouse glaciers of Westland National Park.*
New Zealand is a skier's and climber's paradise particularly as most of the national parks are empty during winter months.

66-67 *Sunset on Mount Cook (foreground) and Mount Tasman (left), the two highest summits in New Zealand. A blanket of cloud in the distance covers the West Coast forests and the Tasman Sea. On Christmas Day 1894 a small party of New Zealanders made the first ascent of Aoraki by climbing the north ridge (left hand rocky skyline) then up the summit icecap.*

68 *Dawn on the 8,200 feet icy rampart of the Aoraki's Caroline face can be enjoyed from an easy-to-reach vantage point on the Furggen ridge above the Tasman Glacier in Mount Cook National Park. The high peak of Aoraki (Mount Cook) is not visible in this photograph being hidden by the Middle Peak* (top right of picture).

69 *This aerial view of the Main Divide Peaks in Mount Cook National Park has been taken during summer from above the Tasman Glacier. Aoraki, New Zealand's highest summit, is visible on the far left of the range.*

70-71 *Sunset on Mount Aspiring can be enjoyed from a vantage point on Mount French above the Bonar Glacier. Mount Aspiring National Park is a major mountain wilderness in the central South Island with easy access from the township of Wanaka. Scenic flights from Wanaka provide another way to enjoy the Southern Alps for those who do not wish to trek into the high mountains.*

72-73 *Buckled and broken by extreme pressure, the Balfour Glacier of Westland National Park cascades over a cliff into gloomy forested gorges beneath the clouds. The setting sun lights up the cloud cover over the Tasman Sea. Storms roll in from the Tasman Sea bringing very high winds and rain during summer months with heavy wet snowfalls in winter. Movement on West Coast glaciers such as the Balfour, Fox and Franz Josef is extremely rapid.*

74 The New Zealand Alpine Club recently constructed this red 20 bunk cabin to celebrate 100 years of the NZAC. The "Centennial" hut is located on the Franz Josef Glacier snow and has already proved popular with ski-mountaineers and climbers. This view of the Franz Josef shows how dramatically the glacier drops away into the gorge under the clouds.
The narrow coastal plain and Tasman Sea can be seen in the distance.

75 Evening light casts a soft purple glow across the crevasses of the Franz Josef Glacier in this view from the balcony outside the New Zealand Alpine Club's new Centennial hut.

76-77 The township of Frankton near Queenstown is dwarfed by the peaks of the Remarkables which are coated in a light autumn snowfall. Lake Wakatipu is a popular resort for yachting.
The Remarkables and nearby Coronet Peak have some of the South Island's best skiing in winter months from June to October.

78-79 For many years the Milford Track has been called "the finest walk in the world". Fiordland National Park has many similar walking routes but there is no question that the Milford, with its modern cabins and well-maintained track, is perhaps the most beautiful, combining launch trips at the start and finish of the trip, easy river flats and a steep though short climb over the spectacular McKinnon Pass.

The bubbling, boiling heart of the North

80-81 *The dramatic colours of the "Champagne Pool" (left) and the sulphur-crusted edges of Whakarewarewa geyser (right) add force to playright George Bernard Shaw's comment after visiting the Rotorua district in 1934 "I was pleased to get so close to Hades and be able to return". Once a visitor has adjusted to the pungent sulphrous smell around Rotorua there is no question the region has many fascinating features centred on the active vulcanism, hot springs and strong Maori culture. "Pohutu", the biggest geyser in New Zealand, thunders into the sky more than 98 feet several times each day. Trout fishing in the crystal-clear waters of Lake Taupo is also a major attraction of the area.*

83 *Tongariro National Park's "Chateau" hotel is tucked under the highest peak in the North Island, the volcano Ruapehu. In the foreground is part of the Chateau's 18-hole golf course. Secluded walking tracks criss-cross the forests which cloak the volcanic slopes of the mountain. Ruapehu's crater lake can exhibit violent eruptions of boiling water and mud. There are several major ski fields on Ruapehu catering for Auckland and Wellington enthusiasts.*

84 *This aerial view of Mount Tarawera illustrates how violent volcanic eruptions can be in this central part of the North Island. The 820 feet chasm almost split the volcano in two. Scenic flights around Rotorua, the Tongariro National Park and over Mount Tarawera provide a new perspective on this ever-changing region. Light aircraft can even land on the summit caldera of Tarawera to allow closer inspection of the crater.*

85 *About twelve miles to the south of Rotorua is a still unspoilt area of hot springs: the Waimangu Valley. In this photograph, one can admire the Emerald Pool, one of the many volcanic lakes that distinguish the entire area.*

86-87 *Muted winter light on the snowy flanks of the dormant volcano Taranaki (Mount Egmont) illuminates old lava flows which carve a path down into forests below. Taranaki is the centrepiece of a rich dairy farming region on the West Coast of the North Island. The mountain often catches violent weather coming in from the Tasman Sea which can be seen in the background of this aerial view.*

Cities in a Tranquil Land

88 top *Lyttelton, Christchurch's port just a few miles from the city over the Port Hills, is as sheltered a harbour as any in the country. From container ships and fishing vessels to private yachts, Lyttelton is a hive of industry, yet on a calm summer's day the harbour is a peaceful place for a family stroll or relaxed lunch in one of the wharf cafés. Lyttelton is rapidly becoming a fashionable place to live for long-time Christchurch residents looking for a change of outlook. Brightly coloured wooden cottages cling to the steep hills rising above the harbour. Pioneering Antarctic voyages in the early 1900s used Lyttelton as a base before finally venturing into the Southern Ocean.*

88 bottom *Taunton Gardens in Governor's Bay near Christchurch was built in 1853. This lovely stone cottage with its magnificent garden typifies many of the historic homes that can be visited in New Zealand.*
The Christchurch and Bank's Peninsula region enjoys a near-perfect growing climate with temperate plants such as roses, rhododendrons and azaleas bursting into flower in the warm spring weather.

89 *Wellington, the nation's capital with its kaleidoscope of multi-coloured roofs, clings to the northern edge of Cook Strait on the tip of the North Island. Suburbs sprawl through rugged bush-clad ridges which descend steeply right into the business and political heart of the city.*

Auckland, the City of Sails

90 *Auckland is by far the biggest city in New Zealand with over one million residents. The city sprawls over an enormous area and in area is almost the size of Sydney. Custom Street is typical of Auckland's business centre and while many high-rise buildings have rocketed up in the last decade, traffic, by world standards, could never be described as heavy. Auckland enjoys a warm temperate climate with hot mid-summer weather enticing many to the region's delightful waterways and nearby islands.*

91 left *Auckland is known all over the world as "The City of Sails", for its superb harbour is the playground for hundreds of yachts, cruising for pleasure or gripped in the throes of a club race.*

91 right *Queen Street is down-town Auckland's business heart, full of modern buildings and fashionable shops. Lunch-time workers enjoy their lunch in the sunshine of Queen Elizabeth Square.*

92-93 *One of Auckland's many marinas for private pleasure craft known as New Haven is only a few miles from the city centre. Ocean-going yachts come to New Zealand for refitting and provisioning before heading north towards the Pacific islands. Skippers often pick up new crews in Auckland for the next leg of their voyage. Next to rugby and football, yachting would be New Zealand's most popular sporting activity. Each year Auckland hosts the "Round the Bays" fun-run which is perhaps the biggest of its kind in the world with up to 100,000 taking part.*

Windy
Wellington

94-95 *Wellington's cable car climbs steeply from the harbour-front city centre to the suburbs around Victoria University. Tree ferns called "pungas" overhang the rails in places. Visitors to Wellington often use the cable car to reach vantage points overlooking the harbour.*

95 *Wellington breeds tough sailors, for although this down town yachting marina looks placid enough, nearby Cook Strait is a storm-tossed stretch of water - certainly no place for the inexperienced. Although Wellington is one of New Zealand's busiest cities, residents only have to travel a few miles before they can relax in open countryside or on a wild coastline.*

96-97 *This aerial view of Wellington gives a good feel for the size and nature of New Zealand's capital city. The business heart of the city is perched on the harbour-front with Parliament House, the circular "bee-hive" visible in the bottom left of the photograph.*

Christchurch, the garden city

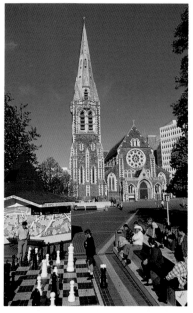

98 top *Playing chess with giant pieces is a popular lunchtime activity in Christchurch's Cathedral Square. Food stalls, concerts and soap box speakers such as the city's very own "wizard" also help to enrich life in the city centre.*

98 bottom *Visitors to Christchurch can escape from their rental car or bus tour to stroll around the museums, art galleries and gardens. Some prefer to sit back and be guided around in the back of a horse-drawn carriage. This view of Christchurch shows the old sandstone building of Canterbury Museum which is located beside the Botanic Gardens.*

99 *The old Canterbury University buildings and courtyards have been turned over to a thriving arts and crafts community who sell their wares in a variety of shops and outside stalls. Buskers, musicians, acrobats and the town crier enliven a Sunday afternoon's entertainment for the whole family.*

Dunedin,
the University City

100 *On the banks of the Leith river The University of Otago dominates the northern end of Dunedin. City life is influenced by the large student population who come from all over the world to study there. With a strong Scottish heritage Dunedin residents have to live with the title of "Dunedin - Edinburgh of the South" though there is* *also a feeling of the English university cities of Oxford and Cambridge as well. Dunedin services a large rural community stretching across Southland and Otago. In the 1860s, following the discovery of gold, Otago experienced a rush of immigrants similar to that of California. Dunedin rapidly became the financial capital of New Zealand.*

101 *St. Kilda beach photographed from St. Clair headland is a popular beach resort town within an easy drive of Dunedin. Wind-blown sheep farms on the Otago Peninsula come to the edge of the headland in the background.*

Living with the Pace of the Land

102 top *New Zealanders love their water sports - be it sailing on Auckland's many bays, skin diving in the Bay of Islands or kayaking down a mountain torrent in the Southern Alps.*

102 bottom *Well-trained sheep dogs assist a South Island farmer herd part of his flock along the road to another paddock. New Zealand was built on the wool and lamb market principally to Europe. Visitors to New Zealand often cannot believe how green the grass is.*

103 *Float planes are an ideal way to get about Lake Te Anau in Southland. Te Anau is also the base for exploration of remote corners of Fiordland National Park, a mountainous wilderness of high alpine peaks, dense vegetation and secluded fiords.*

104-105 *Rotorua bowlers enjoy their game before retiring to the Tudor Towers restaurant for lunch. This fine old building also houses the Rotorua Art Gallery which exhibits work by New Zealand artists such as Rita Angus and Colin McCahon.*

105 *Arrowtown's "Millbrook' Resort" features a golf course designed by New Zealand's famous left-hander Bob Charles. The resort is only a 20-minute drive from Queenstown and Coronet Peak skifield. New Zealand has many great golf courses and many visitors to the country simply come to enjoy the unhurried nature of the game in beautiful surroundings.*

At one with the natural world

106 left *Family camping on the Heaphy Track is the perfect way to spend the Easter weekend. Nikau palm trees dominate the vegetation in this unusually warm micro-climate in the north-west of the South Island. Camping and trekking holidays introduce many young New Zealanders to outdoor life at an impressionable age, allowing them to grow up with the ability to recreate and enjoy simple inexpensive pursuits.*

106 right *This cycle tourer has had to give way to a curious female Hooker's Sea Lion ambling across the road on the Catlin's coast south of Dunedin. These sea lions mainly breed on the sub-antarctic islands south of New Zealand; however, many find their way to South Island beaches. New Zealand is home to many endemic birds and animals making the country a paradise of those keen to observe the natural world.*

107 *New Zealanders are proud that you can drink from virtually any fresh water stream in the country. This young girl is quenching her thirst under Punchbowl Falls in Arthur's Pass National Park west of Christchurch.*

108-109 *The Heaphy Track traverses beautiful forest country in the north west of the South Island: however, the first day on the trail north from Karamea winds along beaches and Nikau palm groves. These shags do not seem to mind the two hikers walking along the edge of the surf.*

Life admist. nature

110-111 *Golden light shines through morning mist on the West Coast's Lake Kanarie as this lone fisherman tries his hand for a breakfast feed. Many such lakes are dotted along the West Coast of the South Island. Fly fishing for trout in mountain streams also attracts a dedicated following of enthusiasts in New Zealand. The brown and rainbow trout were introduced to New Zealand*

in the 19th century. Many luxurious lodges exist in the country to cater for the visitor keen to test his skills with the rod. Some resorts insist that any fish caught is gently released back into the water.

111 *Big game fishing off Painia in the Bay of Islands attracts enthusiasts from all over the world.*

Off the edge of a wave

112-113 *Windsurfing on Canterbury's Lake Coleridge will test even the experts as a strong westerly wind off the Southern Alps rips across the water. New Zealand, being a small group of islands with a myriad of lakes and wild coastlines, is an ideal place for windsurfing.*

113 *Commercial rafting companies take passengers on many of the thrilling mountain rivers spilling down from the peaks of the Southern Alps. For those keener on a slightly tamer experience, rafting and canoeing trips on the meandering Wanganui river in the North Island may appeal. New Zealanders have built up a considerable reputation in recent years for their ability to excel in triathalon, multi-sport competitions, involving mountain running, cycling, canoeing and swimming.*

114 *The Whitbread Round-the-World race is perhaps the toughest test of both yacht and sailor. This aerial view of Auckland harbour shows the fleet departing on the New Zealand - South American leg of the race. The big ocean-going yachts are being farewelled by a flotilla of enthusiastic New Zealanders who have played host to the international crews for ten days while they rest, enjoy "Kiwi" hospitality and have their craft repaired.*

115 *New Zealand yacht designers have built up an impressive reputation in recent years after the performance of their entries in the America's Cup and Whitbread racing events.*

"Kiwi is magic"

116 top *Junior rugby football is played with a fervour and passion throughout the New Zealand school system. An increasing number of girls play both rugby and soccer. Everyone who plays the game aspires to join the ranks of the famous All Black National Rugby Team.*

116 bottom *This young woman is concentrating hard as she puts her horse through its paces at a country agricultural show. Horsemanship has long been an important sport in New Zealand inspired in recent years by the Olympic gold medal winner Mark Todd.*

117 *Country fairs such as this one in Queenstown often have competing axemen chop their way through logs anchored to a baseplate.*

118 *This ski mountaineer has had a long hard climb from the valley floor of the Matukituki river to French Ridge hut. Mount Aspiring National Park in winter holds some very demanding skiing and climbing routes which require skill and experience to handle safely.*

119 *Ski touring in Westland National Park under New Zealand's second highest peak Mount Tasman holds some great delights. Good snow conditions usually exist throughout the winter months from July to October.*
The national parks in New Zealand have an excellent network of high mountain huts which can be used by self-sufficient parties for a very modest cost.

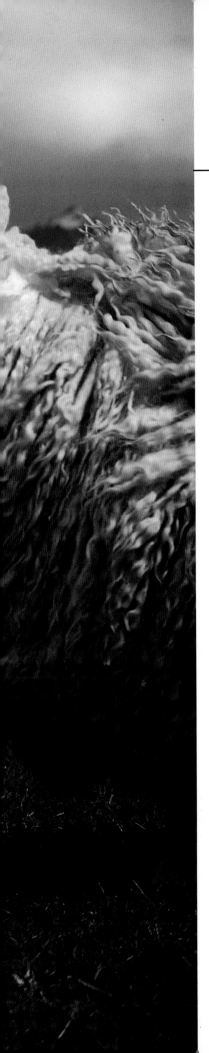

Farming:
a way of life

120 *Spring lambs arrive in late August/September, although in this photograph the ewes have not been shorn before lambing. Early lambs, timed to meet demand for the Christmas market in the Northern Hemisphere, can sometimes be severely affected by snowfall.*

121 top *New Zealand shearers are in demand around the world for their skilful speedy work. Many shearers work on a continual circuit around the world travelling from New Zealand farms to South Africa, Italy, Australia and the Falkland Islands. Women are also employed in shearing gangs some of whom clock up impressive daily tallies solely with hand shears.*

121 bottom *This typical Southland sheep farming landscape gives a feeling for much of the farming country in the lower South Island.*

122-123 *This dairy herd is moving out into a fresh paddock under the Seaward Kaikoura mountains after the morning milking. Dawn light illuminates the peaks and overcast sky.*

The Vikings of the Sunrise

124 and 125 top *The Maori Haka can be as fierce today as it was when the* Pakeha (Europeans) *first faced the war-like Maori in the 1800s. Skilled Polynesian navigators, the Maori landed on the northern coast of New Zealand in their ocean-going* waka (canoes) *some 800 years before the arrival of the first Europeans. Modern Maori still maintain* wakas *taking part in various ceremonies and interisland voyages.*

125 bottom *Maori women get ready to perform their traditional Poi dance in Christchurch to welcome foreign dignatories.*

126-127 *Traditional Maori entrance ways on their* maraes *(courtyard, meeting grounds) are carved in native Totara and Kauri woods. The Maori people still welcome guests onto their* maraes *with a hui ceremony whereby the visitor is called onto the* marae *with a karanga - a long wailing call that beckons the living and celebrates the dead. The* karanga *is performed solely by women. The Maori language and most other aspects of their culture are very much alive in New Zealand today.*

128 *Cigar-shaped clouds forming over the Remarkable mountains above Queenstown are the harbingers of strong wind and heavy rain sweeping in from the Tasman Sea.*

Photo credits:

Pat Barrett / Hedgehog House:
page 44.

M. Bennetts / Hedgehog House:
pages 22-23.

Shaun Bennetts / Hedgehog House:
page 75.

Cargo Borlenghi / Sea and See Italia:
pages 114, 115.

Bouting / Explorer:
pages 120-121.

Markus Brooke / Apa Photo Agency:
pages 103, 111.

Gerald Cubitt / Bruce Coleman:
pages 2-3, 39, 40-41, 56-57, 85.

Nicholas De Vore / Bruce Coleman:
pages 69, 78-79.

Dallas and John Eaton / Apa Photo Agency:
Cover, pages 1, 11, 14-15, 60-61, 121 bottom.

Manfred Gottschalk / Apa Photo Agency:
pages 50, 58-59.

Bruce Jeffries / Hedgehog House:
page 82.

J. Kuglur / Apa Photo Agency:
page 90.

A. Lorgnier / Visa-Cedri:
pages 80, 98 top, 102 bottom, 113, 121 top.

Zim Maori / Hedgehog House:
page 127.

Graeme Matthews / Hedgehog House:
pages 8, 45, 56 center, 125 top.

Colin Monteath / Hedgehog House / Explorer:
pages 28 bottom, 108-109.

Colin Monteath / Hedgehog House:
pages 62-63, 64, 68, 72-73, 74, 76-77, 83, 106, 107, 118, 119, 122-123, 125 bottom.

Brian Moorhead / Hedgehog House:
pages 124-125.

Fritz Penzel / Bruce Coleman:
pages 18-19.

Peter Morath / Hedgehog House:
pages 4-5, 9, 12-13, 16-17, 20-21, 24-25, 26-27, 28 top, 29, 31, 34-35, 36-37, 38, 46-47, 51, 52-53, 54, 55, 56 left, 66-67, 88, 91 right, 94,95, 96-97, 98, 99, 100, 101.

Andrea Pistolesi:
pages 6-7, 42-43, 65, 84-85, 89, 91 left, 92-93, 102 top, 105, 116.

Craig Potton / Hedgehog House:
Back cover, pages 86-87.

Andy Price / Bruce Coleman:
pages 30, 81.

Nathan Secker / Hedgehog House:
pages 110-111, 112-113.

John Shan / Bruce Coleman:
pages 47 right, 48-49.

Roy Sinclair / Hedgehog House:
page 59.

Will Steffen / Hedgehog House:
pages 70-71.

Adina Tovy / Explorer:
pages 32-33, 104-105, 126.

Hugh van Noorden / Hedgehog House:
page 128.

Giancarlo Zuin:
page 117.